# How to Start a House of Worship for the Religious Entrepreneur

## Launch a Church, Ministry, Temple, Mosque, Synagogue & Other Religious Non-Profits in the United States

By

## Robert Langley

**Copyrighted Material**

Copyright © 2019 – **CSBA Publishing House**

Email:csbapublishing@gmail.com

All Rights Reserved.

*No part of this publication may be reproduced, stored in a retrieval system or transmitted in any form or by any means, electronic, mechanical, photocopying, recording or otherwise without the proper written consent of the copyright holder, except brief quotations used in a review.*

Published by:

CSBA Publishing

**CSBA Publishing House**

Cover & Interior designed

By

Jamie Boykin

*First Edition*

# Contents

Forward ................................................................ 7

Introduction ....................................................... 13

Make a Plan ...................................................... 16

    Name ............................................................... 17

    Religious Denomination ............................... 21

    Goals ............................................................... 21

    Brand ............................................................... 22

Set Up a Fund-Raising Platform ...................... 26

    Applying for an EIN ...................................... 27

    Before You Apply .......................................... 29

    How to Open a Church Bank Account ................ 35

    Setting up Donation Platforms ......................... 36

    Applying for a Grant ..................................... 42

Complete the Paperwork ................................. 47

    Certificate of Formation ................................ 48

    501(c)(3) ......................................................... 49

Form a Team ..................................................... 59

    Hire the right people for the geographical area your

church is in. ................................................................. 59

Give each team member clear job descriptions ..... 60

Care about more than your team's work performance ................................................................. 62

Schedule time to do more than just work. ............ 63

Teach each person how to write an annual plan. ..67

Intentionally develop each member of your ministry staff. ................................................................. 67

Don't hold on to anyone too tightly ..................... 68

Draft Bylaws ................................................................. 69

Tips for Writing Bylaws ....................................... 70

Guidelines for Writing Bylaws ........................... 70

Find a Worship Space ................................................. 75

Temporary Beginnings ....................................... 76

Zoning Regulations ............................................. 78

Building Your Own Church ................................. 79

Network For Members ................................................. 85

Inviting Friends ................................................... 86

Host a Party ........................................................ 86

Online Services .................................................. 87

Be on Social Media ............................................... 88

Be Involved ........................................................... 90

Make Invites Easy ................................................ 90

Shareable Invites ................................................. 91

Send Texts ............................................................ 91

Personal Thanks .................................................. 91

Share Stories ....................................................... 92

Address Guests ................................................... 92

Planning Services and Events ................................. 93

Services ................................................................ 93

Planning Church Events ..................................... 96

Grow Your Congregation ....................................... 102

Give a little more thought to your welcome ........ 103

Find ways to attract young people to your church. ........................................................................ 103

Make yourself more accessible. ......................... 104

Get your church involved in the community. ...... 104

Partner with other churches. .............................. 105

Share stories on social media ............................ 105

Speak to your demographic. ...........................105

Think signage. ...............................................106

Use visitor registration cards...........................106

Include your city. ...........................................107

Do community events. ...................................108

Volunteer outside of the church.......................108

Resource List...................................................110

Last Words......................................................113

# Forward

This book is designed to help facilitate your quest, or calling, for religious entrepreneurship.

A religious entrepreneur is an individual who creates an organization that has a religious mission.

Specifically, this book targets those seeking to start a brand new or transitioning house of worship. Whether this religious organization and house of worship is a church, mosque, temple, synagogue, or any other religious structure, this book is for you.

I will give you what you need to start out with establishing, running, and growing a religious organization.

According to the US

government, all religious organizations that are houses of worship are basically just 501(c)(3) entities or tax-exempt non-profits. This not only goes for Christian churches but any organized entity that governs a place of worship.

In this book, the words "church" and "place of worship" are used interchangeably to refer to a place of any religious denomination where people can come to pray or attend a religious service.

Likewise, the terms "parishioner," "church goer," and "congregation" are meant to signify members or attendees of your place of worship, regardless of how your particular group refers to them.

Historically, houses of worship and religious-based entities have been pivotal to the health and function of society.

Religious entities fill in the gaps for public services, providing help, and filling the needs of their members and those less fortunate in the community. Churches provide food, clothing, housing assistance, childcare, vocational assistance, mental health counseling, as well as spiritual advice.

Religious groups tend to take care of their flock best, meeting the needs of those who would be pushed under the rug in society. These groups are often the elderly, homebound disabled people, and families with members who have special needs.

When we think about the natural end of life, often, religious ceremonies and considerations come into play.

The local church or religious community steps in to fill this need as well.

Many important socially beneficial charities have arisen due to the vision of religious entrepreneurs who jumped to fill a need in their community. Some notable organizations include The American Red Cross, The Salvation Army, and the formation of orphanages, which were a religious invention.

Religious leaders have often been influential in their communities. While churches cannot lobby for political influence or back a certain candidate outright, or they risk losing their non-profit status, religious organizations have been able to impart their political beliefs in other ways.

Often, influential faith leaders will begin movements or organizations to spread their message. An example is the National Prayer Breakfast, which puts political and community leaders from all over the world in one room to meet and network – all in the name of faith.

Faith-based initiatives may also include more grass-roots efforts. The Fellowship of Christian Athletes is a way for those school athletes to bond together while sharing the Christian faith. The "See You at the Pole" initiative is a student-led time of expression of faith centered at the school's flagpole.

There are many factors to consider when you think you want to start a religious organization. Thinking about your grand plan and world view would be a good extension of your efforts. Could your church, temple, synagogue, etc. become that influential?

Of course, you are not in this vocation for the money! While money is a big part of the grand scheme of things – and a huge part of any type of business' startup – it is not your focus.

Hopefully, no matter which religion you are, or what sort of faith-based business you want to start, I hope you are considering the broader scope and bigger picture of the impact you will have on your attendees, both physically and spiritually.

If you're going to fall under the purview of an already established religious organization such as the catholic church, for example, you should be familiar with what their individual requirements are for the formation of a gathering place.

Consequently, if you're wanting to start a Jewish synagogue, you must begin with at least 10 Jewish adult males as founding members. You may want your church to belong to a national organization like the Southern Baptist Convention or the United Methodist

Church. Check with these organizations to see what their joining requirements are in addition to the legal regulations listed in this book.

Finally, I must give a special thanks to my long-time friend Lee Stephens. Lee has been a wonderful mentor, spiritual advisor, and a sagacious source of information for me while writing this book. I sincerely appreciate his support.

# Introduction

Have you ever thought of starting your own place of worship? Maybe you're a minister and don't like the church you're at now, or the church is getting ready to close for some reason.

Maybe you feel called to lead your own congregation, or to meet a need of an area that's devoid of access to a house of worship.

Whatever your reason, you may have thought of starting your own place of worship, but don't know how to go about it.

You probably have a lot of questions:

- Where can I have my services?

- Do I have to purchase or lease a huge plot of land?

- What are the legal matters involved?

In this book, we'll cover everything you need to know about how to start a place of worship, including:

- How to make a plan, and the information that should be included in it

- Making a fundraising plan, and the steps you need to take to get your church's finances set up

- Forming a team

- Completing the paperwork, including the certificate of formation and 501(3)(c) form

- Drafting Bylaws

- Finding a Worship Space

- Networking for Members

- Scheduling Services and Events

- Growing Your Congregation

Once you've finished reading this book, you'll know everything you need to know about all the legal aspects of starting a place of worship, finding a worship space, drafting your bylaws, finding members, scheduling services and events, and how to keep your church growing.

# Make a Plan

When you're starting a place of worship, you'll need to make a plan. This plan should include the following details

- The name of the place of worship

- The religious denomination

- The goals you want to accomplish with your place of worship.

- How you want to brand it

We'll talk about each of those details in this

chapter.

## *Name*

The name of any business is important. You want to make sure the name conveys your church's message and reflects the brand. Here are a few ideas for naming your church:

- **Use the church's religious denomination in the name.**

    To make it easy, especially if you know this is the only church of this denomination in the area, you might call it "The (whatever denomination) Church of (whatever area/city). For example, "The Catholic Church of Cabarrus" or "The Cabarrus Catholic Church."

- **Use spiritual lingo in the church name**.

    If you know your church isn't the only one of that denomination in the area, you might want to throw some church lingo in the name to make it stand out from the others.

For example, you could call it something like "Spiritual Unity Catholic Church" or "Baptist Fellowship Church of (your city)." When using spiritual lingo in your church name, remember you want the name to fit on a church sign, so don't make it too long.

- **Use the location of your church in the name.**

If you know your church is the first church of this denomination in the area, you could call it something like "First Baptist Church of (your city)." Make sure the city name will fit well in a church name.

For example, if your church is located in Hell, MI, "The First Baptist Church of Hell" might not be a good church name.

- **Choose a church name that gets people's attention while still reflecting your brand.**

More churches are selecting names

that grab people's attention. Many churches have started using the words Journey, Bridge, Mosaic, and Generation in their names in the past few years. Other words that have been used in church names include Impact, Potential, Epic, Transformation, Renovation, and Innovate.

- **Don't use "church" in your name.**

If you're opening a church in an area that's more of a coffee shop community, consider using the words Village, Community, Center, Assembly, or People in your name.

No matter what you choose to call your church or place of worship, here are a few tips that will help you come up with an appropriate name:

- **Choose a name that has meaning.**

Church names are special and should reflect what your

church wants to accomplish. Choose a name that will give the members of the community something to think about when they see the church.

- **Choose a simple name.**

Church names shouldn't be hard to pronounce or remember.

- **Choose a name that's easy to remember.**

There are almost 400,000 places of worship in America today. Therefore, it's important to choose a name that's original, but also easy to remember.

- **Keep the focus on your higher power.**

While it's important to choose a name people will remember, you also need to choose a name that keeps the focus on God, or whoever your higher power is.

A name like "The (city name) New Life Assembly of God" keeps the focus on God, while also being original.

## Denomination

This one isn't hard. You most likely already know what religious denomination you want your church to be based on.

If you're of a certain religious denomination, but also want to start a church that welcomes people of all religious denominations, that's fine too. It may work well in a city that has people of many different denominations living in it.

## Goals

Every business has certain goals it wants to accomplish, and a church is no different.

Maybe your main goal is to help more people in your community in some way. To help you decide your goals, ask yourself these questions:

- How will you do it?

- What steps will you need to take in order to do it?

- What resources will you need to accomplish this goal?

These are all questions you need to ask yourself when establishing goals for your church.

## Brand

Every business, even non-profits, needs to brand itself. As you figure out the brand for your place of worship, keep these tips in mind:

- **Figure out where you fit in**.

The first thing you need to figure out is who you want to reach in the community. It's impossible to reach everyone, so maybe you want to reach out to a specific section of the community.

Perhaps your focus will be on the people who are poorer and maybe don't go to church as much, because they have a hard time believing in God.

Once you've figured out who you want to help, the next thing you need to figure out is where you fit in.

- **Be specific**.

When you're trying to figure out your

brand, you need to be specific about it.

Consider the following questions when figuring out your church's brand:

- What does your church do?

- What do you want to accomplish in your community?

- Why did you start it?

- Why do people visit your website?

- Who is your ideal parishioner?

- Why do people choose your church over others?

- What other churches do you admire?

- If your church were a person, how would you describe it?

- How do you want people to feel when they visit your church?

- Can you describe your church in 3-5 words?

- What do you love about your church?

- **Be sustainable.**

As your church grows, you'll need to adjust your brand voice to your audience. And you'll have to deliver on the promises you make every day.

- **Be consistent.**

To be consistent, you need to ask a few questions about your church and how it affects your parishioners.

Questions you could ask include:

o How does my church affect my ability to serve my parishioners?

o How does it affect the materials we use to market our church?

o Do the things going on in our community affect the goals I'm trying to accomplish with my church?

o Does it affect the way we answer the phones?

- **Implement changes slowly.**

Once your church has been open for a while and you have a good amount of parishioners, they'll get used to the way you do things.

If you decide to make changes in the future, create a plan to transition your brand slowly. Start with getting a new logo, then a new website, then paint the walls, then get new furniture, then start behaving differently.

Once you change your parishioners' environment, they will adjust to the behavior and brand changes.

Once you've figured out all these parts of your plan, you're ready to move on to the next step - making a fundraising plan.

# Set Up a Fund-Raising Platform

Once you've figured out all the essential details for your church, it's time to figure out how you're going to raise money for your church and talk about the steps you need to take to establish your church finances.

Every business entity requires money, even for a "non-profit" organization.

Every church will have expenses- for the building, utilities, furniture, marketing materials, and computers and software.

In this chapter, we'll talk about the following details:

- Applying for an EIN
- Opening a Church Bank Account
- Setting Up Donation Platforms
- Applying for a Grant

Once you've completed these steps, you'll have your church's finances in place and be able to start bringing in money.

This money helps you expand your church and accomplish the goals you established in the previous chapter.

## *Applying for an EIN*

An EIN, or employee identification number, is a number used by the IRS for businesses and other entities, like churches and non-profits.

Even if you don't have employees, you need to have an EIN so you can apply for a bank account, which we'll be discussing in the next section.

You can apply for an

EIN online at https://www.irs.gov/businesses/small-businesses-self-employed/apply-for-an-employer-identification-number-ein-online or download the PDF form at https://www.irs.gov/pub/irs-pdf/fss4.pdf.

## Before You Apply

Before you apply, make sure you understand everything the form is asking for. You'll have to provide the following information on the form:

- **Legal Name of the Entity**

The name given to the business, or in this case, the name of your place of worship, which you should have decided on in the last chapter.

- **Trade name/Business name**

This is how your church will be known in the community and the name that will be on your sign and any advertising you do. It may or may not be the same as the legal name.

Whatever you decide to use as your trade name, make sure to use the same name, either the trade name or the legal name, on all your filings with the IRS to avoid confusion. Don't use your trade name on one form and the legal name on another.

- **Name of the administrator or trustee**

This is the person who's in charge of legal matters. You'll want to include the social security number, EIN, or ITIN of this person or business.

- **Business mailing address, street address, and county and state where the business is located**.

These are three separate items on the form, but they must be filled out correctly. If you choose to use a PO Box for your business communication, the physical street address of the business will be different from the mailing address.

- **Responsible party**.

The responsible party is the person who "controls, manages, or directs the entity and the disposition of the entity's funds and assets." Basically, they're the person who's responsible for the finances of your church. You'll need to provide this person's EIN.

- **Items 8a, b, and c**

These only apply if you're setting up an LLC (limited liability corporation). If you answer "yes" to Item

8a, you'll have to provide information in items 8b and c.

- **Type of entity**

This is pretty easy unless you're setting up an LLC. If you are, you'll have to decide whether you're a single-member LLC or a multiple-member LLC.

If you're not sure which one you are, ask your income tax professional. Keep in mind, the type of business entity you select is not an official election of your tax type. You'll select a way to pay taxes with a different form.

The following item, 9b, only applies if you're a corporation.

- **The reason you're applying**

If you're establishing a new church or place of worship, you will choose "Started a new business" and provide a brief description of your church.

- **Date business started**

You might want to choose the date you actually opened your doors and started taking parishioners.

- **Closing month of the accounting year**

This is the last month of your accounting year. You can start your financial year whenever you want, although most businesses choose December 31 as the end of their fiscal year.

If you're not sure what to set as the closing month of your accounting year, check with your CPA or tax professional.

- **Item 13**

This line asks you to choose the highest number of employees you expect to hire in the next 12 months. Unless you're running a farm or hiring household help, you put the number under "other."

- **Item 14**

This item asks you if you'll have less than $1,000 in employment tax liability. If you have no employees, or you'll be paying less than $4000 to all employees within the year, mark "no."

- **Item 15**

If you have

employees, enter the estimated date of your first payroll.

- **Item 16**

Enter the business classification for your type of business.

- **Item 17**

Provide more information on the products or services you'll be providing. In the case of a church, you might want to say something like "spiritual guidance."

- **Item 18**

Indicate if this business has ever applied for and received an EIN before. You can include the name of a third party designee to receive your EIN if you don't want to receive it. A lawyer can usually do this for you.

Finally, once you've filled out all the items, sign the form. This shows you believe all the information is true, correct, and complete.

Tips for completing the EIN form:

- **Decide if you will apply online, by phone, mail, or fax.**

Look for information on the IRS website to find out more about the process of applying with each of these methods.

- **If you complete the application online or by phone, you'll receive your EIN immediately.**

Print out the page with the EIN or write it down. You'll need it for many of the applications and documents you'll fill out as you start your church.

If you applied by mail or fax, you'll receive a confirmation in the mail. Be sure to keep it in a safe place.

## *How to Open a Church Bank Account*

Once you have an EIN, you can open a church bank account.

We'll discuss why you need a bank account, the information you'll need to open the account, different donation platforms you can choose, and how to apply for grant money in this section.

**Why do I need a church bank account?**

You need a church bank

account, so you have a place to deposit money collected from offerings, safeguard donations and cash received from fundraisers, deposit tax withholdings, and settle opening costs of running the church.

**Information needed to open a church bank account:**

- A copy of your church's bylaws

- Your EIN

- Statement of Beliefs

- Statement of Faith

- 501(c)(3) certificate to show your church is tax-exempt

- Money to fund the opening balance

Be sure to contact a bank first to find out about their opening requirements. Different banks have different requirements for how much you need to open an account.

## *Setting up Donation Platforms*

One of the best ways to get money for your church is to get it from your parishioners. You can ask for money at your services, but one of the best ways to encourage people to make donations to your church is to use online donation platforms.

Some of the most popular online donation platforms include:

- **Tithe.ly** (https://get.tithe.ly/)

This platform is free unless you want to use text-to-give, which costs $19 a month. Parishioners can give donations through the mobile phones, online giving integrations you can add to your website, kiosk giving, admin gift entry, and text to give. There's a 2.9% fee to use Tithe.ly, plus an additional 30 cent charge for each transaction.

**Advantages of using Tithe.ly**:

It's convenient for your donors. They can give using an app, or through a website integration that doesn't require them to be logged into the website. Tithe.ly accepts ACH bank transfers, credit and debit cards, and manual entry.

It supports recurring gifts and payments. Donors can set up recurring gifts, which helps them establish consistent giving habits.

It includes a "cover the fee" option where donors can select if they want the option to cover the transaction fee as an extra way to support your church.

- **EasyTithe** (https://www.easytithe.com/)

This can be used on mobile phones and Facebook. They also have text-to-give and kiosk options, which have additional fees. You can pay nothing for it, or pay up to $49 a month for it, depending on the plan you choose. The transaction fee charged to your parishioners varies depending on the plan you choose. If you choose the free option, they'll be charged $3 plus an additional 39 cents each time they give.

**Advantages of using EasyTithe:**

If you're looking for something simple, the free option lets your parishioners give from their mobile phones or online. Plus, there's no start-up fee charged to you.

- **MinistryOne app** (https://www.ministryone.com/)

Churches can also download the MinistryOne app, which provides access not only to giving but also to sermons, video, event registration, and streaming video.

It's convenient and easy to use. Donors can set up automatic recurring donations and pay with credit, debit, or ACH.

There's also a cover the fee option. Donors can have the fees automatically added to their donation.

If your church chooses the paid option, it can sell items through EasyTithe's online store option if they choose.

The customer success team helps churches launch online and mobile giving with videos and 1:1 coaching.

- **Givelify** (https://www.givelify.com/)

This can be used on mobile phones, plus it also has online giving integrations, and parishioners can give at kiosks. It's free but does have a 2.9% transaction fee plus parishioners are charged 30 cents per transaction.

**Advantages of using Givelify:**

It's easy to download and set up and add your church's branding. Plus it's easy for donors to give through the app.

Because it's easy to give through the app, it's a great choice whether your church is big or small.

- **PayPal**

(https://www.paypal.com)

Paypal allows donors to give through the website or email, and it's free for donors to set up. There's a 2.2% transaction fee plus a 30 cent charge per transaction for qualifying non-profits.

**Advantages of using PayPal:**

It's easy to set up a donate button. PayPal has a button users can easily add to any website page or embed in an email.

Users can create a custom landing page

with a link unique to their church for their donors to use to give donations.

Donors can set up recurring monthly donations by clicking a simple checkbox.

- **Pushpay**

https://pushpay.com/

Pushpay allows donors to give through a mobile app, online, through text message, or through a kiosk. They have a tiered pricing structure, and the transaction fee varies from 2.5% to 3%, depending on the card type.

**Advantages of using Pushpay:**

It encourages participation. Pushpay built its platform to encourage non-givers to become regular givers eventually.

They provide excellent support and security. They have a large team dedicated to coaching customers through a 60-day launch strategy, plus they provide continuous support. They also update their platform regularly to keep your information safe at all times.

You can use the app

for more than just setting up donation platforms for your donors.

The advanced features of the app allow you to create connection cards, sermon notes, and bible reading plans for your parishioners.

Those are just a few of the donation platforms you can use for your church.

Ultimately, the one you choose is going to depend on your needs and how much you can afford to spend on fees.

## *Applying for a Grant*

After you've applied for an EIN, opened a church bank account, and set up donation platforms, the last thing you'll want to do is apply for grant money for your church.

Why do you want to apply for a grant?

When you're just starting a church and haven't gotten a lot of donations, you may not have a lot of money to use to get your church off the ground. Applying for a grant helps you get some money so you can get your church started. We'll talk about three steps you need to take in this section.

- **Establish yourself as a 501(c)(3) non-profit organization.**

  Before you apply for a grant, you'll want to establish yourself as a 501(c)(3) non-profit organization. Establishing yourself as a non-profit organization makes you eligible to receive grant funding from private organizations and state and federal funding sources.

  There are many steps to setting yourself up as a 501(c)(3) non-profit, which will be discussed in the next chapter.

- **Establish relationships with private foundations serving your community.**

  It's important to connect with foundations that serve your community. Start with those located in your immediate geographic area and move outward.

  Get to know their mission, focus, and projects they've funded in the past. If you can, call them to make an appointment to meet with them in person.

Don't ask for funds right away. Make the first contact about introducing yourself and establishing a relationship.

If you can't meet with them face to face the first time, write a short letter introducing yourself and your organization. Include information on your history, mission, programs you've stated, goals, the people you serve, the reason you're reaching out to their organization, and how you feel your missions are similar. Ask for a time to meet with them and follow up from there.

Think of these relationships as long-term relationships that could build a foundation for your organization.

- **Create a community coalition.**

Your church may already be a hub for community needs and resources, and you may already have connections with other organizations and institutions in your area, both in public and private sectors.

Once your Board of Directors has established its basic needs, like general operating, programming, and capital, you can bring these connections together and establish a coalition.

We will discuss what the Board of Directors is expected to accomplish in a subsequent chapter.

Doing this will give you access to additional funding.

Private foundations have more leeway regarding the types of projects they fund, projects coming from public tax funds have more strict rules. They may need to relate to non-religious activities and be available to the wider community.

Forming a coalition of public and private organizations allows you to identify programs and funders that will best address your community's needs.

Funders love projects with established partners, so it's important to get the relationships started now.

These are the steps

you need to take to make a fund-raising plan to and establish your church finances.

# Complete the Paperwork

■■■■■■■■■■■■■■■■■■■■■■■

Aside from the EIN, which we covered earlier, there are a few other pieces of paperwork you'll have to complete to start your church, including filing a certificate of formation and an application for 501(c)(3) status.

It's a good idea to get an attorney to help you complete these forms, but we'll discuss the details of the different forms in this chapter, so you have a basic understanding of what goes into each form.

## *Certificate of Formation*

A Certificate of Formation makes the church legal in the eyes of the government. It also ensures your church name is unique.

When you file it, you're registering your church as an LLC, or limited liability corporation. Rules for how to complete it will differ depending on your state, but in general, it contains:

- The name of the LLC which should have the words "LLC," "Limited Liability Corporation," or "Limited Liability Company."

- The name and address of the person responsible for receiving service of process should the church become involved in a legal suit.

- The address of your church's main location.

- Whether the LLC is managed by a manager or the members.

You also might need to include:

- The name and address of one or all of the members.

- The addresses and names of the people who organized the church.

- Whether the business is a professional LLC if that designation exists in your state.

- Whether the LLC is a single-member or has multiple members.

- If some or all of the members will be liable for some or all of the obligations, debts, or liabilities of the church.

## 501(c)(3)

Most churches apply for this status with the IRS. These organizations can't be organized to benefit private interests, such as those related to, directly or indirectly controlled by the private interests.

Second, the organizations need to follow the specific

organization and operation guidelines that the IRS identifies in Section 501(c)(3).

Lastly, any of these organizations can't take part in electioneering, campaigning activities or other political activities.

You'll need your EIN to apply for the federal tax-exempt status for your church. To file it, you'll need to go through the following steps:

1. Write an **articles of incorporation** and register them with your state government. Articles of incorporation show that your church is a legal entity that conducts business, accepts donations, and is exempt from paying taxes. Each state has different processes for filing articles of incorporation; you'll have to research the process for your state.

Your church can exist in a few different forms:

- A nonprofit corporation
- A charitable trust

- An unincorporated association

2. File **IRS Form 1023**. You can find this form online at https://www.irs.gov/forms-pubs/about-form-1023. This is the main part of the application, and requires the following components to be submitted along with it:

    - The most recent version of the form
    - A signature from an authorized individual
    - Your EIN
    - A statement of receipts and expenses
    - A copy of your organizing document or charter
    - Detailed narratives of activities you want to organize
    - Your church's bylaws and governing rules

3. Decide whether you're starting a **public charity, a private foundation, or private operating foundation**.

This is important because it affects the forms you'll need to complete to be recognized as a tax-exempt non-profit. It also differs slightly from the first step listed above.

If your organization is a nonprofit corporation, you need to make sure you fill out the correct application for what your non-profit is trying to accomplish.

All potential tax-exempt organizations are considered private foundations unless they are churches, hospitals, schools, or research organizations, or currently have fund-raising programs and receive funds from multiple sources.

So more than

likely, your church would be considered a charitable organization, and you would have to complete Form 1023.

4. Write your **Bylaws** and Decide on Your Programming and Board members ahead of time.

We'll discuss these details in future chapters, but they must be done *before* you submit your 501(c)(3) application, because you need all of them when you submit Form 1023.

The IRS uses them to decide the soundness of your governing and financial framework, guiding mission, and how sustainable your church is.

You'll need to make sure these things are as complete as possible, and focus on certain areas for each:

**Bylaws** - Make sure you include a

complete draft of them; they should already be adopted and active when you submit them with your application.

**Outlines of your first programs** - Explain and describe the programs for your church's first initiatives. You may want to look at it in the same way you would a grant proposal and adjust the scope of your descriptions.

**Your governing structure** - Include the names, addresses, and titles of your founding executive officers and board of directors. If your executive director gets paid, include information on it.

5. Understand the **goals and mission** of your church.

You should create a mission statement for your church that explains it's motivation and the principles that guide it. It should explain the church's principles in a way that others will understand.

Most importantly,

you should be able to defend it.

Developing a mission statement for your church helps you make your case for both support and tax exemption status strong and defensible.

Write out the following for your church:

- Mission statement

- Intentions

- Your plan to accomplish the first goals for your church

- Your key stakeholders and supporters

Thinking about every aspect of your operations and purpose will help you identify any problem areas that might delay your application.

6. Check for any **state-specific requirements**.

    Your state may have certain requirements for the 501(c)(3) application. The most important thing you want to look for is the requirements for registration for charitable solicitation.

Soliciting donations is the most important part of any nonprofit's operations, so you want to know the requirements before you receive tax-exempt status.

You'll also want to research any other specific requirements your state might have for finalizing your tax-exempt status. Some state requirements overlap with the federal requirements for 501(c)(3) status.

You might have to do any of the following in your state:

- Just complete your nonprofit articles of incorporation

- Submit materials showing you've been given federal

501(c)(3) status

- Complete a completely different state process

- Submit different forms with your 501(c)(3) determination letter

7. Be patient and **follow all the tax laws** for non-profit organizations while you wait.

Once you've submitted your application, it can take a while to receive tax-exempt status.

Your approval could be delayed for a few different reasons:

- One or more documents are missing.

- Not enough financial information provided.

- Financial and programming schedules aren't included.

- The wrong

user fee for the application submitted.

The IRS has policies you need to follow while waiting for tax-exempt status, so make sure your team knows what they are and follow the financial reporting steps.

While you're waiting for approval, go ahead and proceed as though you've already been granted tax-exempt status.

Start implementing your programs and following the rules about when you need to report your earnings.

Now that you understand the details you need to provide to complete the paperwork for your church, it's time to talk about forming a team for your place of worship.

# Form a Team

Once you've completed the paperwork for your church, it's time to start working on building your church staff.

But what kind of people should be on your church staff?

We'll provide some tips for selecting the right people for your church staff in this chapter.

*Hire the right people for the geographical area your church is in.*

If your church is in an urban setting, hire

people who love working in an urban setting and feel called to deal with the problems of people living in an urban setting.

Other things you need to consider when hiring the right people for the area your church is located in include:

- community demographics
- ethnic makeup
- economic issues
- church culture
- theological culture

Also remember that just because someone was successful working in one context, it doesn't mean they'll be successful working in yours.

## *Give each team member clear job descriptions.*

The worst thing you can do when hiring people for your church staff is not giving people a clear job description. Everyone should know exactly what they're supposed to do.

The minister of music should know that he's supposed to select the music to play at every service, and whoever's responsible for choosing the readings for each service should be in charge of that.

Whoever's responsible for church finances should only be responsible for keeping track of the income earned from donations, weekly offerings, and anything else the church does to raise funds.

Review the job descriptions every three months with your staff members and make sure it still adequately reflects their duties.

Make adjustments as needed.

## *Pay your team fairly.*

Most churches operate with volunteers who simply provide voluntary, uncompensated services. However, there are also churches who hire employees that have compensation and working conditions based on the federal and state laws.

When you choose to hire an employee you are faced with a number of legal requirements from filing with the state to determining adequate wages/compensation and calculating withholdings for tax purposes.

Even tax-exempt charitable nonprofits (a house of worship) are required to pay minimum wage. A requirement of maintaining tax-exempt status is providing compensation that is reasonable and not excessive.

When hiring a new staff member, you should know what the going rate is by comparing salary and benefits information from other nonprofits in your area with a similar mission.

Employees must be paid the legal minimum wage that varies by state or by the federal minimum wage. Employees should be paid whichever is higher. If employees work over 40 hours a week, a nonprofit may still owe these employees for overtime.

## Care about more than your team's work performance.

Remember that issues in your team's personal life can affect their work performance. Consider asking your team members these questions to get a better idea of what's going on outside work that might be affecting their performance:

- What are you struggling with that affects your ministry or your own personal relationship with Christ?

- What do you need help with?

- How is God changing you right now?

- When you look back over time, what has God changed in you?

- Who is your toughest relationship right now?

- How can I pray for you today?

## Schedule time to do more than just work.

It's important that you schedule some time for recreation as a staff. Maybe schedule your staff to run a 5k, or do something else fun together. Get ideas from your team, and allocate funds in the church budget for it.

Some ideas you could try include:

1. **Having an ice cream party.** This one works especially great during the summer. You could keep the freezer in your office stocked with ice cream or ice cream treats, or host a full-fledged ice cream social for your staff.

2. **Flip Flops.** During the summer, buy pairs of flip flops for your staff in fun colors. If you don't know their shoe sizes, you can estimate them. The average man's size is 10 1/2, and the average woman's size is 8 1/2. Allow them to trade pairs until they get the color and fit they like.

3. **Movie Under the Stars.** This would be a fun one to do with your staff and their families. Arrange to show an outdoor movie, and choose a good family-friendly movie,

like The Sandlot, Frozen, or any Toy Story movie. Kids can come in their pajamas and fall asleep, and parents can enjoy a drive-in movie.

4. **Afternoon Sweet Tea or Lemonade break.** Buy a few gallons of sweet tea or lemonade and let your staff have a sweet tea or lemonade break on a Friday afternoon. It's a great way to cool off during summer, and a great way for your staff to socialize for a bit. During the winter, you could substitute coffee or hot chocolate for sweet tea and lemonade.

5. **Funday Friday.** Let your staff leave at noon on a Friday afternoon if they don't have a lot to do.

6. Take your staff and their families to a **baseball game.** This is a great one, especially if you live near a city that has a Major League Baseball

team. Even if you don't live near a city that has a Major League Baseball team, minor league games can be just as fun to watch and less expensive.

7. **Serve watermelon**. Serve watermelon at a staff meeting or as a mid-morning snack. You could make things even more fun by having a watermelon seed spitting contest.

8. **Infused water and Outdoor Staff Meeting.** On nice days, set up tables and chairs outside for your next staff meeting. Depending on how long your meeting is, you might want to set them up in the shade or provide sunscreen for your staff members. You can serve homemade infused water at the meeting. Your staff will definitely enjoy the treat and the opportunity to be outside.

9. **Water gun fight or a snowball fight.** You may have to set boundaries for this one, but a water gun fight can definitely make the day more fun, especially during the hot summer months.

## *Teach each person how to write an annual plan.*

An annual plan helps any business, including a church, figure out what their problems are and how they can fix them, and what goals they want to accomplish in the coming year.

Each person should write an annual plan for their specific duties, then all the individual plans can be combined into one big plan for the year.

## *Intentionally develop each member of your ministry staff.*

As a church leader, one of your jobs is to develop each member of your staff.

Figure out what you're going to do to develop the strengths of each member of your team, and make sure each person knows that you're committed to their growth.

Part of your legacy will be the kingdom's impact on the people who follow behind you.

## Don't hold on to anyone too tightly.

Eventually, each member of your team may want to branch out and do other things. Some may become pastors, others may want to start their own churches. Don't hesitate to let them go when it's time for them to move on and do something else. Your church will be taken care of after they leave.

In the next chapter, we'll talk about drafting bylaws for your church.

# Draft Bylaws

Your church's bylaws establish your church's rules, explain how elections are run, define the different leadership positions, what missions the church participates in, the programs it runs, and other important matters.

Before you write your

bylaws, nominate people from the community who want to become church members or people who already belong to the church.

## *Tips for Writing Bylaws*

Bylaws are put in place to make the church less susceptible to crisis situations.

Because of this, they need to be clearly written.

If you choose to act as a non-profit organization, be sure you write the bylaws before you send your application for incorporation to the state or federal government.

## *Guidelines for Writing Bylaws*

Meet with the church board to talk about the bylaws and decide your church's focus. The secretary should take notes from this meeting.

- Write down the official name and collect bank documents, bills, bank accounts, and other important documents.

- Define the purpose and what you want to address in your ministries, and decide your legal status.

- For example, is your church a registered tax-exempt non-profit, or do you have a different tax status? This is important because it helps you define how you operate in terms of donations.

- Discuss your church's religious denomination. If it belongs to a specific denomination, mention it in the bylaws. This will help guide the statement of faith for your church, or the beliefs your congregation has.

- Write your church's mission statement and decide how your leaders will accomplish the church's goals. What kind of outreach programs or projects will you do?

- Discuss your church's membership requirements, including the steps to become a member and each member's rights, and what they have to do to remain members, if applicable. Include whether they'll be able to vote on issues, or if the board only has voting rights.

- Decide how staff members are chosen or elected and their responsibilities within the congregation. Clearly outline how the process will work.

- Decide on the rules for board meetings. These should spell out who has voting rights at the meetings, how they are regulated, and how often the board should get financial updates.

- Decide what departments your church will have. These should include areas your church is interested in. For example, if you want to minister to youth, you might consider having a youth ministry department. If you want to minister to women, you could have a women's ministry department.

- Discuss whether the church should own land or other resources, and decide if they'll be listed under the name of the church or one of the staff members. Churches have to follow the laws in each state. In some states, churches have to be incorporated and own land. If the church is in a state that requires this, and decides not to incorporate, then one person should have the assets in their name.

- Explain the steps that will be taken to make changes to the church's bylaws, and if a majority of the members need to decide to change them. As the church gets bigger, the bylaws may need revision.

- Plan for the possibility that the church has to close. Decide the division of assets in the event it does close.

- Approve the bylaws with a vote. If most of the board members approve them, they will help the church run smoothly.

That's it for this chapter, in the next chapter, we'll talk about finding a worship space for your church.

# Find a Worship Space

Another important thing you need to do when starting a place of worship is finding a place to hold services.

Depending on how much your church has to start with, you may not be able to find a place to build a church right away. This means you'll have to get creative with finding places to hold your services and events if you choose to have those right away.

Also, you may have to find a place to hold board meetings in the beginning. In this chapter we'll discuss a few places you can hold church services and church meetings and then go into how a church should be designed once you do have space for an actual church.

## *Temporary Beginnings*

When you first start, you may be limited on the places you can use for your church services. However, you still want to try to find a place to hold your church services that will accommodate your entire congregation.

Some places you might consider looking at for your church worship services include:

1. **Schools**. Talk to school personnel to see if they'll let you rent space in their school to use for your church services. This can be difficult if the school is using the space for other purposes, but if they're not, they may rent the space to you for a small fee. Contact the school district

to see if they can work with you on it.

2. **Movie Theaters**. Many movie theater chains rent space to churches. Some chains, like Regal and Cinemark, have church starting programs and consultants who will work with church staff on renting out theater rooms for Sunday morning worship services. It costs more to rent space in a movie theater, but there's better parking, and set-up crews don't have to worry about clean-up because the movie theater takes care of that themselves.

3. **Gyms, Karate Dojos, or Dance Studios**. If you need a lot of empty space, talk to a gym or karate dojo. These places usually have limited hours on Sundays, so they may be open to creating extra income by renting out their space to

a church when they're not open. There's usually a lot of parking space, but you may have to bring your own chairs. It usually costs less to rent these spaces than it does to rent space in a school or theater, but it can sometimes be difficult to find space and utilize it well in a gym. Also, if the gym has a lot of heavy equipment, it may not be suitable.

4. **Restaurants**. There may be restaurants near you that are closed on Sundays, or at least on Sunday mornings. Check with them and see if they would be willing to rent space to you to use for your services during these times. It can be tough to find space in a restaurant, but if you can find one that has plenty of room, you won't have to worry about chairs.

## *Zoning Regulations*

When considering where to hold religious services, you may have to consider zoning laws. Some states and localities have places limits on where congregations can meet.

Check with your local city or county government for local zoning ordinances before you close the deal on your new church property.

There also may restrictions on renovating an old church building due to historic preservation laws. It's a good idea to do your research when picking a suitable church building location.

Here is a good article with further information regarding zoning laws: http://plannersweb.com/wp-content/uploads/2012/08/457.pdf

## *Building Your Own Church*

Once you've made enough from donations to start thinking about finding a larger worship space, you might think about building a church. When you're building a church, there are certain details you want to keep in mind about the architecture.

- **Steeple.** The steeple traditionally served three functions. The steeple's vertical lines directed prospective parishioners' eyes toward the heavens, which made the church more visually appealing.

  Also, most church buildings were short and fat, so a steeple helped make it look more visually pleasing. Finally, the steeple was usually the most noticeable structure in an area as it allowed people to locate the church anywhere in town.

- **Church bells.** The church bells are found inside the steeple. They were mainly rung to let people know when it was time for church. However, they could also be used to let people about a fire or an army that's approaching.

- **Nave.** This part is the main center part of a Christian church. It goes from the entrance of the church to the pulpit.

- **Chancel.** Some churches conducted services from the chancel. It usually has a platform for the pastor and the choir. Some churches don't have a separate nave and chancel.

- **Baptistry.** Baptisms were performed in the baptistry until the 6th century. This area was connected to the church, or close to it.

By the 10th century, baptismal fonts had replaced baptistries because baptisms were being performed by pouring water over someone's head. Baptist churches and other churches that use immersion baptism built special baptistry pools into the chancel's wall or floor.

- **Altar/Communion Table**. The altar is the table in the chancel that's used for communion. During the Reformation, some people started calling the altar the communion table because they felt the name "altar" was misleading.

  Anglicans decided both terms were correct, because we get Jesus Christ's sacrifice from the altar, and because it's the table Communion is performed on. Today, Anglicans and Lutherans call it the altar, while churches of other Protestant faiths refer to it as a communion table.

- **Stained glass windows**. Stained glass was made using metallic oxide or baked in a kiln after colors had been painted on it. Stained glass windows became popular during the middle of the 1100s.

These windows created a heavenly light, symbolizing God's presence, and taught Bible stories to parishioners who couldn't read. Stained glass windows became less popular during the Reformation, but became popular again during the mid-1800s.

- **Pulpit.** The preacher stands on this platform when giving his sermon. Until the Reformation, most pulpits were found on the congregation's left side. During and after the Reformation, pulpits were moved to the center of the sanctuary to emphasize the importance of God's word.

- **Religious symbols like a cross or crucifix.** Catholic churches use a representation of the cross, which they call a crucifix, with an image of Jesus suffering.

In contrast, most Protestant churches show an empty cross; this symbolizes Jesus was overcoming his suffering and death and rising again. Lutheran churches are the exception to the rule. They sometimes display a crucifix, and sometimes don't.

In any case, you could consider using some sort of religious imagery for whatever your higher power is considered to be.

That wraps up the chapter on finding a worship space, and elements to keep in mind when you decide to establish your own church in your own space. In the next chapter, we'll talk about tactics you can use when networking for members.

# Network For Members

Once you've got all the legal paperwork finished and found a space to hold church services, it's time to start networking for members.

You may have already found some people who would be interested in joining during these beginning stages, but you need to find ways to keep growing your church so you can keep spreading your message.

In this chapter, we'll

discuss some ways to network for members.

## *Inviting Friends*

Encourage the people you already have in your church to bring someone they know.

Nothing is more powerful than word of mouth when starting any new business, including a church. People are more likely to respond to an invitation if it comes from someone they know, rather than a mailing sent to their home or an email sent to their inbox from a source they don't know.

Current members can provide comfort and make them feel less isolated when they first come to the church.

## *Host a Party*

One of the easiest ways to encourage your current members to bring a new member is to make it easy for them to do it. A friends and family day provides an opportunity for you to show your current members' friends and family members what your church has to offer.

In the days leading up to the event, give your

current members materials they can share with others, like cards or flyers.

If you know a lot of your members have email, you might even put together some kind of online message they can email their friends and family.

On the day of the event, find ways to encourage people to come back the following week.

One thing you could do is begin a series of sermons that all relate to one another. Make the sermon interesting enough that people will want to come back next week to find out the content of the next sermon.

In the days after the event, reach out to the people that came and let them know how much you enjoyed having them there. Make them want to come back for the next service.

## Online Services

A great way to spread your word to those who might want to get to church but can't for whatever reason is to stream your services over the Internet. It's also a great way to reach potential members who want to see what your church services are like before they attend an actual service.

One thing many pastors worry about with streaming services, however, is that it will affect in-person attendance on Sunday mornings.

Streaming can actually grow and strengthen your church for a few reasons:

- It shows you understand your members' lifestyles.

- It can be used as a teaching tool.

- It can keep your members connected.

- It improves your church's Google ranking and SEO (search engine optimization) score

## *Be on Social Media*

Twitter, Facebook, and other social media networks let you connect with people in many different ways. Use these platforms to share inspirational content, post updates about your church and events you have planned, and share recordings of the live streams of your sermons.

Your current members can share these posts with their social networks, which amplifies your ministry's impact and spreads your message farther.

You could also encourage members to use social media during the service.

This may sound counterproductive, but if you encourage members to share status updates or tweets during the service, you'll increase church attendance because members will be able to provide real-time updates about the service.

Create content other members can share.

Sometimes it's scary for other members to invite their friends and family to church. Create helpful content that will be easy for other members to share on their social networks.

Some ideas include inspirational posts, links to helpful articles, or a list of local restaurants where kids eat free. We'll provide a link with some examples in the resources list at the end of this book.

Write Facebook posts your members can share.

Instead of asking them to make up their own Facebook posts, create one that they can easily share with their Facebook followers. Create one they can copy and paste, and include an image with it.

## Be Involved

Challenge people to get involved in the issues your church is addressing that mean the most to them.

People who are passionate about the message you're spreading will want your work to be successful, so they'll probably invite others to join them and help spread your message even farther.

## Make Invites Easy

Give your members invitations they can give to their friends and family to encourage them to come to the church. This can be a ticket sized card, a pamphlet, or a simple business card.

## Shareable Invites

Make an invite page on your website. Create a page that has graphics, sample Facebook posts, and ideas members can use to invite their friends. Tell your members and donors to visit the page for ideas.

## Send Texts

Members who have cell phones might appreciate receiving a text message reminder about church services or upcoming events. You can send these to your regular attenders as well as volunteers at the church and ask them to bring a friend with them.

You can check out the tool Text in Church (https://textinchurch.com/) to easily send text messages to your members and volunteers.

## Personal Thanks

When someone brings a friend to church, send the member a note and thank them personally for inviting them. It could read something like "Sally came to church on Sunday and said you were the one that invited her. Thank you for extending an invitation to her."

## Share Stories

Tell stories about inviting. There's no better way to get the message across about inviting people than by telling stories about invitations during your church service.

## Address Guests

Try to address new members during your sermon. If you create a series of sermons around a certain theme, provide context for any guests that may be present.

Now that you've got some ideas for how to network for members, it's time to start scheduling services and events.

# Planning Services and Events

Now that you've got your church established and figured out how to attract members, it's time to start thinking about planning services and events.

When planning services and events, there are several things you need to consider. We'll discuss those considerations in this chapter.

## Services

In the past, the traditional trend has

been to schedule one service at 11:00 am. However, that trend is changing. Those churches will soon be in the minority. Many churches have started planning their service times differently.

**Many churches have started scheduling multiple Sunday morning services.** This used to be common only with larger churches. However, smaller churches have started doing this, as well.

**Many churches are not holding 11:00 am worship services anymore.** This change started slowly but is more widespread now. Many churches are now holding services at earlier times, usually between 7:00 and 8:30 am, probably because of the number of baby boomers who no longer have children in the house.

**More churches are scheduling services on days other than Sunday.** The growth in this trend is steady, so this may become common in many churches soon.

**More churches are scheduling concurrent worship services.** In other words, they've either got more than one person preaching services at the same time, or they've got a video feed going while they preach their services so people can watch from other places.

**The most popular worship services are starting between 9:30 and 10:30 am.** This time attracts people to churches that have both single and multiple worship services.

**Disagreements over worship times will continue to decrease.** As more churches schedule different worship times, disagreements over worship times will continue to go down.

**Find out from your staff what times they think different members of the congregation will attend, then schedule your services at those times.**

**If you find certain worship times aren't working, ask your congregation what worship times would work for them.** If your congregation mostly consists of younger members, the 11:00 am worship service may not be convenient for them. You could try sending out a survey to your congregation asking them what days and times would be most convenient, then schedule your services on those days and times.

**Consider offering streaming services so people who can't be there in person can watch from home or from another location.** This may not be possible in the beginning, but as your church grows, it could be something to consider.

**Look at scheduling services during the week if Sunday isn't a good day for most church members.** Many people have other obligations on Sunday. They may have to work, or they have family members to take care of. If this is true for a lot of your members, consider scheduling a service during the week if that would be more convenient for them.

## *Planning Church Events*

It's also important to plan events other than church services. Church events could serve a variety of different purposes. They could provide fellowship, a way to reach out to the community, or raise money for a cause your church supports.

There are several steps you should take when planning an event.

**Decide on the goal of the event.** As mentioned above, church events can be held for a variety of reasons. It could be a way for your church members to mingle with one another, a way to reach out to the community, or raise money for a cause. Once you've decided on the goal of the event, you'll be able to plan it effectively.

**Decide how much you can spend on the event.** Before you can start planning, you need to know how much you can spend on the event. You also need to know if you'll be raising any money at the event.

When making your event budget, you'll need to consider things like the cost of marketing, decorations, food, entertainment, equipment you may have to rent, and supplies. As you list all of these things, determine how much you're willing to spend on them based on the amount of money you have in your budget for church events.

**Decide on your event's theme.** Your event theme helps determine all the other aspects of the event. It also creates an atmosphere and should be used during the entire event.

**How do you want to market your event?** You also need to decide how you're going to get the word out. Part of this will be determined by how much money you have in your budget for marketing.

If your marketing budget is very small, you may want to stick to posting information on your church website and in the church bulletin. If you have more money in your budget and want to get the word out to a larger audience, you could print out brochures or advertise on local radio and TV stations. Regardless, think about who your target audience is and look at how much money you have to spend on marketing.

**What activities do you want to have at the event?** Activities are what make church events fun. If you're having a church picnic, you may want to come up with games for adults and children, or if you're having a trivia night, you may want to come up with questions pertaining to your theme. Again, when planning activities, you'll need to think about supplies, instructions, and how the prizes are awarded, among other things.

**What kind of food do you want to serve?** Food is the biggest highlight of any event. When thinking about food, you'll need to decide whether you want to cater the event or have volunteers from your congregation prepare food. The food should center around your theme, and you'll need to make sure you provide plenty of plates, napkins, cups or glasses, and silverware.

**Who's going to set up and tear down the event?** Setting up and tearing down the event is the most important part of the event. You'll need to decide who's going to set up the event, including any electricity that's going to be run or tents that need to be put up. If you're hiring an event company to help with the event, they may take care of this themselves, or you may want to have members of your church congregation do it.

**Who's going to decorate for the event?** Decorations require some creative thought and skill at laying, hanging, or designing decorations. These small touches can make a church event memorable.

**What are everyone's job duties going to be?** Once you've gotten people to agree to help with the event, you need everyone to be clear on what their duties are.

The easiest way to do this is to create an organizational chart that shows who the event coordinator is, and who's responsible for each aspect of the event, including marketing, food, decorations, set-up, tear down, and event activities. The resources section contains a link to a church event planning checklist, which has an example organizational chart.

If you follow all the steps and suggestions in this chapter, your members should be happy with your church service times and the events you plan. As you plan services and events, be sure to consider any feedback you get from them so you can make adjustments as needed for future services and events.

# Grow Your Congregation

Now that you've figured out when you want to hold services and what kind of events your members like, you need to start working on ways to keep your church growing.

As with any business, the key to any successful church is to work on continuing to find ways for your church to keep flourishing so you can keep helping your community.

We'll talk about some

ways you can do that in this chapter.

## Give a little more thought to your welcome.

This may seem too simple, but working on how you welcome your guests on Sunday morning makes a difference. Think of the things new churchgoers may be worried about when they attend your church.

- They may wonder whether they'll know anyone.
- Where they should sit.
- If they're dressed correctly.

Try to make your new members feel welcome by learning their names. Just this small gesture can increase the chance they'll return to your church next Sunday by as much as 79%.

They may also appreciate receiving a personal note, whether you mail it to their home or send it to their email.

## Find ways to attract young people to your church.

Many millennials say they don't attend church services because they don't connect with the message. Because of this, more churches are starting to create programming that appeals to young people.

Giving young members leadership positions also shows them how powerful worship is, which increases the possibility that religion becomes important to them.

When children and teens are excited about going to church, they'll tell their family and friends about it.

## *Make yourself more accessible.*

As we mentioned earlier, offering live streaming and church services at different times increases the possibility that more people will come to your church.

## *Get your church involved in the community.*

There are many ways you can get your church congregation involved in your community. You could volunteer to do yard work in a certain neighborhood, serve coffee at neighborhood bus stops, or do community service projects at a nearby elementary school. These projects depend on what your goal is for your church.

## *Partner with other churches.*

This could work well, especially if you're a small church.

If there's another church in your community that has a similar mission, partner with them to do fun community events like Easter egg hunts or summer movies and barbecue nights.

## *Share stories on social media.*

These could be stories about people that have been baptized into the church, or other stories of things that have happened in people's lives since they joined the church.

## *Speak to your demographic.*

Figure out what your ideal demographic is and plan your sermons, outreach programs, and promotional materials to suit that demographic.

If you want your church

to attract young urban professionals, for example, you'd want to plan sermons and music that's going to appeal to them and come up with outreach programs they'll want to participate in. If you're not sure how to reach out to your target demographic, ask the current members of your church for suggestions.

## Think signage.

Use your signage and your staff to communicate clearly with visitors to your church.

Visiting a church can be difficult for people who have never attended before. They might be afraid they'll do something wrong and embarrass themselves.

For this reason, make sure your signs clearly point out where they're supposed to go. If your church doesn't have any signs, make sure the staff lets them know where they're supposed to go.

## Use visitor registration cards.

Give your visitors an incentive to return

visitor cards.

One church gave visitors an incentive to return visitor cards by promising that every visitor who returned a visitor card would have a donation made to a local nonprofit in their name. The money was donated in the visitor's name on the same day, and by Monday, the visitor received a personal thank you note from the non-profit for the donation.

Because of the success of the incentive, the pastor saw a 95% increase in visitor card returns. It also showed visitors that the church was generous and knew local nonprofits well. Since they made the change, 80% of their visitors have become regular members.

## *Include your city.*

Bring elements of your city into your church. If you bring in elements from the city your church is located in, it will make your church feel like home to your visitors.

One church did this by using elements from their city in their marketing materials. They also incorporated cultural elements, like

Spanish, into their worship music. They also looked for different ways to connect with the community. When the community has a gathering, the church is there to add value. They might provide free food, bleacher cushions, or hand out water.

## *Do community events.*

Find ways for your church to add value to community events.

You could hand out water or Gatorade during sporting events, or provide tents to get out of the sun. You could even do something as simple as allowing people to park in your church parking lot when parking isn't available anywhere else for an event.

## *Volunteer outside of the church.*

Find ways to get people involved in volunteer opportunities.

Share volunteer opportunities with visitors. Many churches have found sharing these opportunities right away makes visitors likely to return. You might appoint staff people to greet new members and ask questions to identify areas they might be interested in.

These are just a few ways you can keep growing your church community. Incorporate the ways that best fit your church's goals, and your church community will keep growing year after year.

# Resource List

I mentioned several resources throughout this book. Below you'll find links to many of them. I hope they're useful when you're building your place of worship.

**Giving Platforms**

Tithe.ly

EasyTithe

Givelify

PayPal

Pushpay

**Other Resources for Building your Place of Worship**

Text in Church

Regal Church Starting Program

Cinemark Church Starting Program

Church Bylaws Sample

Sample Church Job Descriptions

Church Team Building Activities

Form 1023

Information on State-by-State Filing Requirements for Nonprofits

Additional Church Branding Tips

Sample Church Business Plan

Church Event Planning Checklist

Ideas for Shareable Social Media Posts

**SBC**
http://www.sbc.net/BecomingSouthernBaptist/ActionSteps.asp

**Starting an Islamic Center, free ebook:**
http://www.muslimsi.com/wp-content/uploads/2013/10/How-to-Start-a-Masjid.pdf

**Church of Scientology:** https://www.scientology.org/

# Last Words

Farewell, Religious Entrepreneurs!

Thank you for reading this book. I am glad to see you are interested in furthering your mission as you see it.

We examined the tough aspects of start-up, including how to begin from the flames of inspiration, to garnering funding, to how to grow and keep members.

To qualify as a church under IRS rules, you must structure your organization to comply with the legal definition of a "church."

A "church" must have:

- A particular creed and form of worship
- At least one established place of worship
- A regular congregation
- Regular services
- Ordained ministers

A religious organization that fails to comply with the legal definition of a church can still qualify for tax benefits as a "religious organization," but certain legal benefits will not apply.

Churches are required to operate primarily for religious purposes. They must also refrain from substantial political lobbying activity, and from supporting particular any particular candidate for public office.

Whether you're starting a temple, church, synagogue, mosque, or any other religious organization, I hope this book has helped you in your religious entrepreneurship.

Cross denominationally, the struggle of starting a brand new religious organization is the same.

Would you do me a huge favor?

Would you please leave a review where ever you purchased this book?

I take your comments to heart and will certainly use them to make my writing efforts better.

Thank you so much! I wish you the best in your endeavors.

www.ingramcontent.com/pod-product-compliance
Lightning Source LLC
Chambersburg PA
CBHW070656220526
45466CB00001B/468